REPRINT OF THE OFFICIA[L]

CONSTITUTION

OF

THE STATE OF ALABAMA,

As Revised and amended by the Convention assembled at Montgomery on the Fifth day of November, A. D. 1867.

PREAMBLE.

We, the people of the State of Alabama, by our Representatives in Convention assembled, in order to establish justice, insure domestic tranquilty, provide for the common defence, promote the general welfare, and secure to ourselves and to our posterity the rights of life, liberty, and property, invoking the favor and guidance of Almighty God, do ordain and establish the following Constitution and form of government for the State of Alabama:

ARTICLE I.

DECLARATION OF RIGHTS.

That the great, general and essential principles of liberty and free government may be recognized and established,

WE DECLARE:

§1. That all men are created equal; that they are endowed by their Creator with certain inalienable rights; that among these are life, liberty, and the pursuit of happiness.

§2. That all persons resident in this State, born in the United States, or naturalized, or who shall have legally declared their intention to become citizens of the United States, are hereby declared citizens of the State of Alabama, possessing equal civil and political rights and public privileges.

§3. That all political power is inherent in the people, and all free governments are founded on their authority, and instituted for their benefit; and that, therefore, they have, at all times, an inherent right to change their form of government, in such manner as they may deem expedient.

§4. That no person shall be deprived of the right to worship God according to the dictates of his own conscience.

§5. That no religion shall be established by law.

§6. That any citizen may speak, write, and publish his sentiments on all subjects, being responsible for the abuse of that liberty.

§7. That the people shall be secure in their persons, houses, papers and possessions from unreasonable seizures or searches, and that no warrant shall issue to search any place, or to seize any person or thing without probable cause, supported by oath or affirmation.

§8. That in all criminal prosecutions, the accused has a right to be heard by himself and counsel, or either; to demand the nature and cause of accusation; to have a copy thereof; to be confronted by the witnesses against him; to have compulsory process for obtaining witnesses in his favor; and in all prosecutions by indictment or information, a speedy public trial, by an impartial jury of the county or district in which the offence was committed; and that he shall not be compelled to give evidence against himself, or be deprived of his life, liberty or property, but by due course of law.

§9. That no person shall be accused or arrested, or detained, except in cases ascertained by law, and according to the forms which the same has prescribed; and that no person shall be punished but by virtue of a law established and promulgated prior to the offence, and legally applied.

§10. That no person shall, for any indictable offence, be proceeded against criminally by information, except in cases arising in the land and naval service, or in the militia when in actual service, or by leave of the court for oppressions or misdemeanor in office: Provided, That in cases of petit larcency, assault, assault and battery, affray, unlawful assemblies, vagrancy, and other misdemeanors, the General Assembly may by law dispense with a grand jury, and authorize such prosecutions and proceedings before Justices of the Peace, or such other inferior courts as may be by law established.

§11. That no person shall for the same offence be twice put in jeopardy of life or limb.

§12. That no person shall be debarred from prosecuting or defending, before any tribunal in the State, by himself or counsel, any civil cause to which he is a party.

§13. That the right of trial by jury, shall remain inviolate.

§14. That in prosecution for the publication of papers investigating the official conduct of officers or men in public capacity, or when the matter published is proper for public information, the truth thereof may be given in evidence; and that in all indictments for libel, the jury shall have the right to determine the law and the facts under the direction of the court.

§15. That all courts shall be open, that every person, for any injury done him in his lands, goods, person or reputation, shall have a remedy by due process of law; and right and justice shall be administered without sale, denial, or delay.

§16. That suits may be brought against the State, in such manner and in such courts, as may be by law provided.

§17. That excessive fines shall not be imposed, or cruel punishment inflicted.

§18. That all persons shall, before conviction, be bailable by sufficient sureties, except for capital offences, when the proof is evident or the presumption great. Excessive bail shall not, in any case, be required.

§19. The privilege of writ of *habeas corpus* shall not be suspended, except when necessary for public safety in times of rebellion or invasion.

§20. That treason against the State shall consist only in levying war against it, or adhering to its enemies, giving them aid and comfort, and that no person shall be convicted of treason, except on the testimony of two witnesses to the same overt act, or his own confession in open court.

§21. That no person shall be attainted of treason by the General Assembly; and that no conviction shall work corruption of blood, or forfeiture of estate.

§22. That no person shall be imprisoned for debt.

§23. That no power of suspending laws shall be exercised, except by the General Assembly, or by its authority.

§24. That no *ex post facto* law, or any law, impairing the obligation of contracts shall be made.

§25. That private property shall not be taken or applied for public use, unless just compensation be made therefor; nor shall private property be taken for private use, or for the use of corporations, other than municipal, without the consent of the owner: Provided, however, That laws may be made securing to persons or corporations, the right of way over the lands of either persons or corporations, and for works of internal improvement, the right to establish depots, stations, and turnouts; but just compensation shall, in all cases, be first made to the owner.

§26. That all navigable waters shall remain forever public highways, free to the citizens of the State, and of the United States, without tax, impost or toll imposed; and that no tax, toll, impost or wharfage shall be demanded or received from the owner of any merchandise or commodity, for the use of the shores, or any wharf erected on the shores, or in, or over the waters of any navigable stream, unless the same be expressly authorized by the General Assembly.

§27. That the citizens have a right, in a peaceable manner, to assemble together for the common good, and to apply to those invested with the power of government, for redress of grievances, or other purposes, by petition, address or remonstrance.

§28. That every citizen has a right to bear arms in defence of himself and the State.

§29. That no person who conscientiously scruples to bear arms, shall be compelled to do so, but may pay an equivalent for personal service.

§30. That no standing army shall be kept up, without the consent of the General Assembly; and, in that case, no appropriation for its support shall be for a longer term than one year and the military shall, in all cases and at all times be in strict subordination to the civil power.

§31. That no soldier shall, in time of peace be quartered in any house, without the consent of the owner; or in time of war, but in a manner to be prescribed by law.

§32. That no title of nobility, or hereditary distinction, privilege, honor, or emolument, shall ever be granted or conferred in this State; that no property qualification shall be necessary to the election to or holding of any office in this State, and that no office shall be created, the appointment to which shall be for a longer time than during good behavior.

§33. That emigration from this State shall not be prohibited; and that no citizen shall be exiled.

§34, That temporary absence from the State shall not cause a forfeiture of residence once obtained.

§35. That no form of slavery shall exist in this State; and there shall be no involuntary servitude, otherwise than for the punishment of crime, of which the party shall have been duly convicted.

§36. The right of suffrage shall be protected by laws, regulating elections, and prohibiting, under adequate penalties, all undue influences from power, bribery, tumult or other improper conduct.

§37. That this State has no right to sever its relations to the Federal Union, or to pass any law in derogation of the paramount allegiance of the citizens of this State to the Government of the United States.

§38. That this enumeration of certain rights shall not impair or deny others retained by the people.

ARTICLE II.

STATE AND COUNTY BOUNDARIES.

§1. The boundaries of this State are established and declared to be as follows—that is to say: Beginning at the point where the thirty-first degree of North latitude crosses the Perdido river; thence East, to the Western boundary line of the State of Georgia; thence along said line to the Southern boundary line of the State of Tennessee; thence West along the Southern boundary line of the State of Tennessee, crossing the Tennessee river and on to the second intersection of said river by said line; thence up said river to the mouth of Big Bear Creek; thence by a direct line to the Northwest corner of Washington county, in this State, as originally formed; thence Southerly, along the line of the State of Mississippi, to the Gulf of Mexico; thence eastwardly, including all islands within six leagues of the shore to the Perdido river, and thence up the said river to the beginning.

§2. The General Assembly may, by a two thirds vote of both Houses thereof, arrange and designate boundaries for the several counties of this State, which boundaries shall not be altered, except by a like vote. But no new counties shall be hereafter formed of less extent than six hundred square miles; and no existing county shall be reduced to less extent than six hundred square miles; and no new county shall be formed which does not contain a sufficient number of inhabitants to entitle it to one Representative under the ratio of representation existing at the time of its formation, or unless the county or counties from which it is taken shall be left with the required number of inhabitants entitling such county or counties to separate representation

ARTICLE III.

DISTRIBUTION OF POWERS OF GOVERNMENT.

§1. The powers of the government of the State of Alabama shall be divided into three distinct departments, each of which shall be confided to a separate body of magistracy, to-wit: Those which are legislative to one, those which are executive, to another, and those which are judicial to anoher.

§2. No person or collection of persons being of one of those departments shall exercise, power properly belonging to either of the others, except in the instances hereinafter expressly directed or permitted.

ARTICLE IV.

LEGISLATIVE DEPARTMENT.

§1. The Legislative power of this State shall be vested in a General Assembly, which shall consist of a Senate and House of Representatives.

§2. The style of the laws of this State shall be: "Be it enacted by the General Assembly of Alabama." Each law shall contain but one subject, which shall be clearly expressed in its title; and no law shall be revised or amended unless the new act contain the entire act revised, or the section or sections amended; and the section or sections so amended shall be repealed.

§3. Senators and Representatives shall be elected by the qualified electors on the Tuesday after the first Monday in November. The term of office of the Senators shall be four years, and that of the Representatives two years, commencing on the day after the general election.

§4. No person shall be a Representative unless he is eligible as an elector to vote for members of the General Assembly.

§5. No person shall be a Senator unless he be eligible as an elector to vote for members of the General Assembly, and shall be twenty-seven years of age, and shall have resided for two years within the State, and for the last year thereof within the district for which he shall be chosen.

§6. The House of Representatives, when assembled, shall choose a Speaker and its other officers; and the Senate shall choose a president, in the absence of the Lieutenant Governor, and its other officers; each House shall judge of the qualifications, elections and returns of its own members, but a contested election shall be determined in such manner as shall be directed by law. The President of the Senate and the Speaker of the House of Representatives shall remain in office until their sucessors are elected and qualified.

§7. A majority of each House shall constitute a quorum to do business, but a smaller number may adjourn from day to-day, and may compel the attendance of absent members, in such manner and under such penalties as each House may provide.

§8. Each House may determine the rules of its own proceedings, punish members for disorderly conduct, and, with the consent of two-thirds, expel a member; but not a second time for the same cause; and shall have all other powers necessary for a branch of the legislature of a free and independent State.

§9. Each House, during the session, may punish by imprisonment, any person not a member, for disrespectful or disorderly behavior in its presence, or obstructing any of its proceedings: Provided, That such imprisonment shall not at any time exceed forty-eight hours.

§10. Each House shall keep a journal of its proceedings, and cause the same to be published immediately after its adjournment, excepting such parts as in its judgment may require secrecy, and the yeas and nays of the members of either House on any question, shall, at the desire of one tenth of the members present, be entered on the journals.—Any member of either House shall have liberty to dissent from, or protest against any act or resolution, which he may think injurious to the public or an individual, and have the reasons of his dissent entered on the journals.

§11. Members of the General Assembly, shall, in all cases, except treason, felony or breach of the peace, be privileged from arrest; and they shall not be subject to any civil process during the session of the General Assembly, nor for fifteen days next before the commencement and after the termination of each session.

§12. When vacancies occur in either House, the Governor, or the person exercising the powers of the Governor, shall issue writs of elections to fill such vacancies.

§13. The doors of each House shall be open, except on such occasions as in the opinion of the House, may require secrecy.

§14. Neither House shall, without the consent of the other, adjourn for more than three days, nor to any other place than that in which they may be sitting.

§15. Bills may originate in either House, and be amended, altered or rejected, by the other; but no bill shall have the force of law, until on three several days it be read in each House, and free discussion be allowed thereon, unless in case of urgency, four-fifths of the House in which the bill shall be depending, may deem it expedient to dispense with this rule. And every bill, having passed both Houses, shall be signed by the Speaker and President of their respective Houses: Provided, That all bills for raising revenue shall originate in the House of Representatives, but the Senate may amend or reject them as other bills.

§16. Every bill or resolution having the force of law, to which the concurrence of both houses of the General Assembly may be necessary, except on a question of adjournment, which shall have passed both Houses, shall be presented to the Governor, and if he approve he shall sign it; if not, he shall return it with his objections to the House in which it shall have originated, who shall enter the objections at large on the journals, and proceed to reconsider it. If after such reconsideration, a majority of the whole number of members of that House shall agree to pass it, it shall be sent together with the objections to the other House, by which it shall be reconsidered, and if approved by a majority of the whole number ot members of that House, it shall have the same effect as if it had been signed by the Governor; but in all such cases the votes of both Houses shall be taken by yeas and nays, and the names of persons voting for and against the bill or resolution shall be entered on the journals of both Houses respectively. If the bill or resolution shall not be returned by the Governor within five days (Sundays excepted) after it shall have been presented to him, it shall have the same force and effect as if he had signed it, unless the General Assembly by its adjournment prevent its return, in which case it shall not be a law.

§17. Every order, resolution or vote, to which the concurrence of both Houses may be necessary (except on questions of adjournment, and for bringing on elections by the two Houses) shall be presented to the Governor, and before it shall take effect, be approved by him, or being disapproved, shall be re-passed by both Houses, according to the rules and limitations prescribed in the case of bills.

§18. Each member of the General Assembly shall receive from the public treasury such compensation for his services as may be prescibed by law; but no increase of compensation shall take effect during the session at which such increase shall have been made.

§19. No Senator or Representative shall, during the term for which he shall have been elected, be appointed to any civil office of profit under this State, which shall have been created, or the emoluments of which shall have been increased during such term, except such office as may be filled by election by the people.

§20. No person who holds any lucrative office under the United States, or under this State, or any other State or Government, (except Postmasters, officers in the militia, to whose office no annual salary is attached, Justices of the Peace, members of the Court of County Commissioners, Notaries Public, and Commissioners of Deeds;) no person who has been convicted of having given or offered any bribe to procure his election to any office; no person who has been convicted of bribery, forgery, perjury, or other high crime, or misdemeanor, which may be by law declared to disqualify him; and no person who has been a collector, or holder of any public moneys, and has failed to account for and pay over to the Treasury all sums for which he may be by law accountable, shall be eligible to the General Assembly.

§21. The General Assembly shall meet annually, on such day as may be by law prescribed, and shall not remain in session longer than thirty days, except by a vote of two-thirds of each House.

§22. In all elections by the General Assembly, the members shall vote *viva voce*, and the votes shall be entered on the journals.

§23. All State officers may be impeached for any misdemeanor in office, but judgment shall not extend further than removal from office, and disqualification to hold office, under the authority of this State. The party impeached, whether convicted or not, shall be liable to indictment, trial and judgment, according to law.

§24. The House of Representatives shall have the sole power of preferring impeachment. All impeachments shall be tried by the Senate; the Senators, when sitting for that purpose, shall be on oath or affirmation; and no person shall be convicted under an impeachment without the concurrence of two-thirds of the Senators present.

§25. It shall be the duty of the General Assembly to pass such laws as may be necessary and proper to decide differences by arbitrators, to be appointed by the parties who may choose that mode of adjustment.

§26. It shall be the duty of the General Assembly, from time to time, as circumstances may require, to frame and adopt a penal code, founded on principles of reformation.

§27. It shall be the duty of the General Assembly, within five years after the adoption of this Constitution, and within every subsequent period of ten years, to make provision by law for the revision, digesting and promulgation of all the public statutes of this State, both civil and criminal.

§28. The General Assembly shall have power to pass such penal laws as they may deem expedient, to suppress the evil practice of duelling.

§29. It shall be the duty of the General Assembly to regulate by law, the cases in which deductions shall be made from the salaries of public officers for neglect of duty in their official capacities, and the amount of such deductions.

§30. Divorces from the bonds of matrimony shall not be granted but in the cases by law provided for, and by suit in Chancery; but decisions in Chancery for divorce shall be final, unless appealed from in the manner prescribed by law, within three months from the date of the enrollment thereof.

§31. No money shall be drawn from the Treasury but in pursuance of an appropriation made by law; and a regular statement and account of the receipts and expenditures of all public moneys shall be published annually, in such manner as may be by law directed.

§32. The General Assembly shall not borrow or raise money on the credit of this State, except for purposes of military defence against actual or threatened invasion, rebellion or insurrection, without the concurrence of two-thirds of the members of each House; nor shall the debts or liabilities of any corporation, person or persons, or other States be guarantied, nor any money, credit or any other thing be loaned or given away, except by a like concurrence of each House; and the votes shall, in each case, be taken by the yeas and nays and be entered on the journals.

§33. The States shall not engage in works of internal improvement; but its credit in aid of such, may be pledged by the General Assembly on undoubted security by a vote of two-thirds of each House of the General Assembly.

§34. It shall be the duty of the General Assembly to make adequate provisions in each county for the maintenance of the poor of this State.

§35 Any citizen of this State who shall, after the adoption of this Constitution, either in or out of this State, fight a duel with deadly weapons, or send, or accept a challange so to do, or act as a second, or knowingly aid or assist in any manner those thus offending, shall be incapable of holding any office under this State.

§36. The General Assembly shall not have power to authorize any municipal corporation to pass any laws contrary to the general laws of the State, nor to levy a tax on real and personal property to a greater extent than two per centum of the assessed value of such property.

§37. In the event of annexation of any foreign territory to this State, the General Assembly shall enact laws extending to the inhabitants of the acquired territory, all the rights and privileges which may be required by the terms ot the acquisition anything in this Constitution to the contrary notwithstanding.

ARTICLE V.

EXECUTIVE DEPARTMENT.

§1. The Executive Department shall consist of a Governor, Lieutenant Governor, Secretary of State, Auditor, Treasurer, and Attorney General, who shall be chosen by the electors of the State, at the time and places at which they shall vote for Representatives.

§2. The Governor, Lieutenant Governor, Secretary of State, Treasurer, and Attorney General shall hold their officers for the term of two years, and the Auditor for the term of four years.

§3. The returns of every election for the officers named in the preceding section, shall be sealed up and transmitteed to the Seat of Government, by the returning officers, directed to the presiding officer of the Senate, who, during the first week of the session shall open and publish the same in the presence of a majority of the members of the General Assembly; the person having the highest number of votes, shall be declared duly elected, but if two or more shall be highest and equal in votes for the same office, one of them shall be chosen by the joint vote of both Houses. Contested elections for Executive officers shall be determined by both Houses of the General Assembly, in such manner as shall be prescribed by law.

§4. The supreme executive power of this State shall be vested in the Governor.

§5. He shall take care that the laws are faithfully executed.

§6. He may require information in writing, from the officers in the Executive Department, upon any subject relating to the duties of their respective offices.

§7. He shall communicate at every session, by message to the General Assembly, the condition of the State, and recommend such measures as he shall deem expedient.

§8. He may, on extraordinary occasions, convene the General Assembly by proclamation, and shall state to both Houses, when assembled, the purposes for which they have been convened.

§9. In case of disagreement between the two Houses, in respect to the time of adjournment, he shall have power to adjourn the General Assembly to such time as he may think proper, but not beyond the regular meetings thereof.

§10. He shall be Commander-in-Chief of the military and naval forces of the State, except when they shall be called into the service of the United States.

§11. He shall have power after conviction, to grant reprieves, commutations and pardons for all offences, (except treason and cases of impeachment,) upon such conditions as he may think proper, subject, however, to such regulations as to the manner of applying for pardons as may be prescribed by law; but such pardons shall not relieve from civil or political disability. Upon conviction of treason, he may suspend the execution of the sentence, and report the same to the General Assembly at the next meeting, when the General Assembly shall either pardon, commute the sentence, direct its execution, or grant further reprieve, He shall communicate to the General Assembly, at every regular session, each case of reprieve, commutation, or pardon granted, stating the name and crime of the convict, the sentence, its date, and the date of the commutation, pardon, or reprieve, with his reasons therefor.

§12. There shall be a Great Seal of the State, which shall be kept and used by the Governor officially, and the seal heretofore in use shall continue to be the great seal of the State until another shall have been adopted by the General Assembly.

§13. All grants and commissions shall be issued in the name and by the authority of the State of Alabama, sealed with the Great Seal, signed by the Governor, and countersigned by the Secreeary of State.

§14. No member of Congress, or other person, holding office under the authority of this State, or of the United States, shall execute the office of Governor, except as herein provided,

§15. In case of the death, impeachment, resignation, removal, or other disability of the Governor, the powers and duties of the office, for the residue of the term, or until he shall be acquitted, or the disability removed, shall devolve upon the Lieutenant Governor.

§16. The Lieutenant Governor shall be President of the Senate, but shall vote only when the Senate is equally divided, and in ease of his absence or impeachment, or when he shall exercise the office of Governor, the Senate shall choose a President *pro tempore*.

§17. If the Lieutenant Governor, while executing the office of Governor, shall be impeached, displaced, resign, or die, or otherwise become incapable of performing the duties of the office, the President of the Senate shall act as Governor until the vacancy is filled or the disability removed: and if the President of the Senate for any of the above causes shall be rendered incapable of performing the duties pertaining to the office of Governor, the same shall devolve upon the Speaker of the House of Representatives.

§18. Should the office of Secretary of State, Auditor, Treasurer, or Attorney General, become vacant from any of the causes specified in the fifteenth section of this Article, the Governor shall fill the vacancy until the disability is removed, or a successor elected and qualified. Every such vacancy shall be filled by election at the first general election that occurs more than thirty days after it shall have occurred, and the person chosen shall hold the office for the full term fixed in the second section of this article.

§19. The officers mentioned in this article shall, at stated times, receive for their services a compensation to be established by law, which shall neither be increased nor diminished during the period for which they shall have been elected.

§20. The officers of the Executive Department and of the public institutions of the State, shall, at least five days preceding each regular session of the General Assembly, severally report to the Governor, who shall transmit such reports with his message to the General Assembly.

§21. A Sheriff shall be elected in each county by the qualified electors thereof, who shall hold his office for the term of three years, unless sooner removed, and shall not be eligible to serve either as principal or deputy for any two successive terms. Vacancies in the office of Sheriff shall be ffiled by the Governor as in other cases; and the person appointed shall continue in office until the next general election in the county for sheriff, as by law provided.

ARTICLE VI.

JUDICIAL DEPARTMENT.

§1. The Judicial power of the State shall be vested in the Senate sitting as a Court of Impeachment, a Supreme Court, Circuit Courts, Chancery Courts, Courts of Probate, such inferior Courts of Law and Equity to consist of not more than five members, as the General Assembly may from time to time establish, and such persons as may be by law invested with powers of a judiccial nature,

§2. Except in cases otherwise directed in the Constitution, the Supreme Court shall have appellate jurisdiction only, which shall he co-extensive with the State, under such restrictions and regulations not repugnant to this Constitution, as may from time to time be prescribed by law: Provided, That said Court shall have power to issue writs of injunction, mandamus, habeas corpus, quo-warranto, and such other remedial and original writs as may be necessary to give it a general superintendence and control of inferior jurisdiction.

§3. The Supreme Court shall be held at the seat of Government, but if that shall have become dangerous from an enemy, or from disease, it may adjourn to a different place.

§4. The State shall be divided by the General Assembly into convenient circuits, each of which shall contain not less than three nor more than eight connties, and for each circuit there shall be chosen a Judge, who shall, after his election or appointment, reside in the circuit for which he shall have been chosen.

§5. The Circuit Court shall have original jurisdiction in all matters, civil and criminal within the State, not otherwise excepted in the Constitution, but in civil cases only when the matter or sum in controversy exceeds fifty dollars: Provided, however, That the Circuit Court shall have equity jurisdiction concurrent with the Courts of Chancery in all cases for divorce, and cases in which the value of the matter in controversy does not exceed the sum of five thousand dollars.

§6. A Circuit Court shall be held in each county in the State at least twice in every year, and the Judges of the several Circuits may hold Courts for each other when they deem it expedient, and shall do so when directed by law: Provided, That the Judges of the several Circuit Courts shall have power to issue writs of injunction returnable into Courts of Chancery.

§7. The General Assembly shall have power to establish a Court or Courts of Chancery with original and appellate jurisdiction. The State shall be divided by the General Assembly into convenient Chancery Divisions, and the Divisions into Districts; and for each Division there shall be a Chancellor, who shall, after his election or appointment, reside in the Division for which he shall have been elected or appointed.

§8. A Chancery Court shall be held in each county at a place therein, to be fixed by law, and the Chancellors may hold courts for each other, when they deem it expedient.

§9. The General Assembly shall have power to establish in each county within the State, a Court of Probate, with general jurisdiction for the granting of letters testementary and of administration, and for orphans' business: and the General Assembly may confer on the said courts, jurisdiction of contracts for labor, and order frequent sessions for that purpose.

§10. The Judges of the Supreme Court, Circuit Courts, and Courts of Chancery, shall, at stated times, receive for their services a compensation which shall not be diminished during their continuance in office; but they shall receive no fees or perquisites, nor hold any office (except judicial offices) of profit or trust under this State, or the United States, during the term for which they have been elected, nor under any other power during their continuance in office.

§11. Judges of the Supreme Court, and Chancellors, Judges of the Circuit and Probate Courts, and of such other inferior courts as may be by law established, shall be elected by the qualified electors of the respective counties, cities, towns or districts, for which said courts may be established, on the Tuesday after the first Monday in November of each year, or such other day as may be by law prescribed. Vacancies in the office of the Circuit Judge, Judge of Probate, or Judge of any other inferior court established by law, shall be filled by the Governor: and the person appointed by him shall hold office until the next election day appointed by law for the election of Judge, and until his successor shall have been elected and qualified.

§12. The Judges of the several Courts of this State shall hold their office for the term of six years: and the right of any Judge to hold his office for the full term hereby prescribed, shall not be affected by any change hereafter made by law in any Circuit or District, or in the mode or time of election; but for any willful neglect of duty, or any other reasonable cause which shall not be sufficient ground of impeachment, the Governor shall remove any Judge on the address of two-thirds of each House of the General Assembly: Provided, That the cause or causes for which said removal may be required, shall be stated at length in such address, and entered on the journals of each House: And provided further, That the Judge intended to be removed, shall be notified of such cause or causes, and shall be admitted to a hearing in his own defence, before any vote for such address; and in all such cases the vote shall be taken by yeas and nays and be entered on the journal of each House respectively.

§13. A competent number of Justices and Constables shall be elected in and for each county by the qualified electors thereof who shall hold office during such terms as may be prescribed by law. Said Justices shall have jurisdiction in all civil cases wherein the amount in controversy does not exceed one hundred dollars. In all cases tried before such Justices the right of appeal shall be secured by law: Provided, That Notaries Public appointed according to law shall be authorized and required to exercise, throughout their respective counties, all the powers and jurisdiction of Justices of the Peace.

§14. The Judges of the Supreme Court shall, by virtue of their offices, be conservators of the peace throughout the State; as also the Judges of the Circuit Courts within their respective Circuits, and the Judges of the inferior Courts within their respective counties.

§15. The Clerk of the Supreme Court shall be appointed by the Judges thereof, the Registers in Chancery, by the Chancellor of the Divisions, and all the Clerks and Registers so appointed shall be removed by the appointing power for cause to be placed on the records of the Court.

§16. The Attorney General shall reside at the Seat of Government, and shall be the law officer of the State. During the session of the General Assembly, he shall furnish to the Committees of either House when required, drafts of bills and written opinions upon any matter under consideration of the Committees, and shall perform such other duties as may be required of him by law.

§17. A Solicitor shall be elected in each county in this State by the qualified electors of such county, who shall reside in the county for which he is elected, and perform such duties as may be required of him by law. He shall hold office for a term of four years, and in case of vacancy, such vacancy shall be filled by the Judge of the Circuit until his successor is elected and qualified.

§18. Clerks of the Circuit Court and such inferior Courts, as may be by law established, shall be elected by the qualified electors in each county for the term of six years, and may be removed from office for cause and in such manner as may be by law prescribed. Vacancies in the office of Clerk shall be filled by the Judge of the Court, until the next general election and until a successor shall be elected and qualified. Provided: That the General Assembly shall have power to annex the duties of Clerk to the office of Judge of any of the inferior Courts by law established.

§19. The style of all processes shall be "*The State of Alabama*,', and all prosecutions shall be carried on in the name and by the authority of the State of Alabama, and shall conclude "against the peace and dignity of the same."

ARTICLE VII.

ELECTIONS.

§1. In all elections by the people, the electors shall vote by ballot.

§2. Every male person, born in the United States, and every male person who has been naturalized, or who has legally declared his intention to become a citizen of the United States, twenty-one years old or upward, who shall have resided in this State six months next preceding the election, and three months in the county in which he offers to vote, except as hereinafter provided, shall be deemed an elector: Provided, That no soldier, or sailor, or marine in the military or naval service of the United States, shall hereafter acquire a residence by reason of being stationed on duty in this State.

§3, It shall be the duty of the General Assembly to provide, from time to time, for the the registration of all electors, but the following classes of persons shall not be permitted to register, vote or hold office: 1st. Those who during the late rebellion, inflicted, or caused to be inflicted, any cruel or unusual punishment upon any soldier, sailor marine, employee or citizen of the United States, or who, in any other way, violated the rules of civilized warfare. 2d. Those who may be disqualified from holding office by the proposed amendment to the Constitution of the United States known as "Article XIV," and those who have been disqualified from registering to vote for delegates to the Convention to frame a Constitution for the State of Alabama, under the act of Congress "to provide for the more efficient government of the rebel States," passed by Congress March 2, 1867, and the acts supplementary thereto, except such persons as aided in the reconstruction proposed by Congress, and accept the political equality of all men before the law: Provided, That the General Assembly shall have power to remove the disabilities incurred under this clause. 3d. Those who shall have been convicted of treason, embezzlement of public funds, malfeasance in office, crime punishable by law with imprisonment in the penitentiary, or bribery. 4th. Those who are idiots or insane.

§4. All persons before registering, must take and subscribe the following oath: I ———, do solemnly swear (or affirm) that I will support and maintain the Constitution and laws of the United States, and the Constitution and laws of the State of Alabama; that I am not excluded from registering by any of the clauses in Sec. 3, Article 7, of the Constitution of the State of Alabama; that I will never countenance or aid in the secession of this State from the United States; that I accept the civil and political equality of all men; and agree not to attempt to deprive any person or persons, on account of race, color, or previous condition, of any political or civil right, privilege or immunity, enjoyed by any other class of men; and furthermore, that I will not in any way injure, or countenance in others any attempt to injure, any person or persons on account ot past or present support of the Government of the United States, the laws of the United States, or the principle of the political and civil equality of all men, or for affiliation with any political party.

§5. Electors shall, in all cases except treason, felony, or breach of the peace, be privileged from arrest and civil process during their attendance at elections, and in going to and returning from the same.

§6. It shall be the duty of the General Assembly to enact adequate laws giving protection against the evils arising from the use of intoxicating liquors at elections.

§7. Returns of elections for all civil officers elected by the people, who are to be commissioned by the Governor, and also for the members of the General Assembly, shall be made to the Secretary of State.

ARTICLE VIII

REPRESENTATION.

§1. The House of Representatives shall consist of not more than one hundred members, who shall be apportioned by the General Assembly among the several counties of the State according to the number of inhabitants in them respectively; and to this end the General Assembly shall cause an enumeration of all the inhabitants of the State to be made in the year 1875, and every ten years thereafter, and shall make an apportionment of the Representatives among the several counties at the first regular session after each enumeration; which apportionment, when made, shall not be subject to alteration until after the next census shall have been taken; Provided, That each county shall be entitled to at least one Representative; And, provided further, That when two or more adjoining counties shall each have a residum, or fraction, over and above the ratio then fixed by law, which fractions, when added together, equal, or exceed that ratio, in that case, the county having the largest fraction shall be entitled to one additional Representative.

§2. Until the General Assembly shall make an apportionment of the Representatives among the several counties after the first enumeration made as herein provided, the counties of Autauga, Baldwin, Bibb, Blount, Butler, Calhoun, Clay, Clarke, Cherokee, Cleburne, Crenshaw, Choctaw, Coffee, Conecuh, Coosa, Covington, Dale, DeKalb, Elmore, Fayette, Henry, Jefferson, Lauderdale, Limestone, Marshall, Marion, Monroe, Morgan, Pike, Randolph, St. Clair, Shelby, Walker, Washington and Winston, shall have one Representative each; the counties of Chambers, Franklin, Greene, Hale, Jackson, Lee, Lawrence, Macon, Pickens, Russell, Talladaga, Tallapoosa and Tuscaloosa, shall be entitled to two Representatives each; the counties of Barbour, Bullock, Lowndes, Madison, Marengo, Perry, Sumter and Wilcox, shall be entitled to three Representatives each; the counties of Dallas, Mobile and Montgomery shall be entitled to five Representatives each: Provided, That in the formation of new counties the General Assembly may apportion to each its proper representation.

§3. The whole number of Senators shall be not less than *one-fourth* or more than *one-third* of the whole number of Representatives; and it shall be the duty of the General Assembly, at its first session after the making of each enumeration, as provided by section 1st, of this article, to fix by law the number of Senators and to divide the State into as many Senatorial Districts as there are Senators; which Districts shall be as nearly equal to each other as may be in the number of inhabitants, and each shall be entitled to *one* Senator and no more: Provided, That no county shall be divided, and no two or more counties, which are separated entirely by a county belonging to another District, shall be joined in one District: And Provided, further, that the Senatorial Districts when formed, shall not be changed until after the next enumeration has been taken.

§4. At the first general election after each new apportionment, elections shall be held anew in all the Senatorial Districts. The Senators elected when convened at the next ensuing session of the General Assembly, shall be divided by lot into two classes, as nearly equal as may be: the seats of the Senators of the first class shall be vacated at the expiration of two years, and those of the second class at the expiration of four years, from the day of election, so that (except as above provided,) one half of the Senators may be chosen biennially.

§5. Until the General Assembly shall divide the State into Senatorial Districts as herein provided, the Senatorial Districts shall remain as follows: 1st District. Limestone and Lauderdale; 2d, Franklin and Lawrence; 3d, Morgan, Blount, Winston and Marion; 4th, Madison; 5th, Jackson, Marshall and DeKalb: 6, Cherokee and Calhoun; 7. Walker, Jefferson, and St. Clair; 8, Shelby and Bibb; 9, Tuscaloosa and Fayette; 10, Talladaga and Clay; 11th, Chambers, Randolph and Cleburne; 12th, Coosa and Tallapoosa; 13th, Lee; 14th, Macon; 15th, Russell; 16th, Bullock; 17th, Barbour; 18th, Autauga and Elmore; 19th, Montgomery; 20th, Lowndes; 21st, Dallas, 22d, Perry; 23d, Hale: 24th, Greene and Pickens; 25th, Sumter; 26th, Marengo; 27th, Choctaw, Clarke and Washington; 28th, Mobile; 29th, Monroe and Baldwin; 30th, Wilcox; 31st, Butler and Conecuh; 32nd, Covington, Crenshaw and Pike; 33d, Coffee, Dale and Henry.

§6. Until a new apportionment of representatives to the Congress of the United States shall have been made, the Congressional Districts shall remain as stated in the Revised Code of Alabama, and after each new apportionment, the General Assembly shall divide the State into as many Districts as it is allowed Representatives in Congress, making such Congressional Districts as nearly equal in the number of inhabitants as may be.

ARTICLE IX.

TAXATION.

§1. All taxes levied on property in this State shall be assessed in exact proportion to the value of such property: *Provided, however*, That the General Assembly may levy a Poll Tax not to exceed one dollar and fifty cents on each Poll, which shall be applied exclusively in aid of the Public School Fund.

§2. No power to levy taxes shall be delegated to individuals or private corporation.

ARTICLE X.

MILITIA.

§1. All able-bodied male inhabitants of this State, between the ages of eighteen years and forty-five years, who are citizens of the United States, or have declared their intention to become citizens of the United States, shall be liable to military duty in the militia of this State; but all citizens of any denomination whatever, who from scruples of conscience may be averse to bearing arms, shall be exempt therefrom, upon such conditions as may be prescribed by law.

§2. The General Assembly shall provide for the organizing, arming, equiping, and discipline of the militia, and for paying the same, when called into active service, in such manner as it shall deem expedient, not incompatible with the laws of the United States.

§3. Officers of the militia shall be elected or appointed, and commissioned in such manner as may be provided by the General Assembly.

§4. The Governor shall be Commander-in-Chief of the army and navy of this State, and of the militia, except when called into the service of the United States, and shall have power to call forth the militia to execute the laws, to suppress riots, or insurrections, and to repel invasion.

§5. The Governor shall nominate, and by and with the consent of the Senate, appoint one Major General and three Brigadier Generals. The Adjutant General, and other staff officers to the Commander-in-Chief, shall be appointed by the Governor, and their commissions shall expire with the Governor's term of service. No commissioned officer shall be removed from office except by the Senate, on the recommendation of the Governor, stating the grounds on which such removal is recommended, or by the decision of a court martial pursuant to law.

§6. The militia may be divided into two classes, to be designated as "volunteer militia" and reserve militia," in such manner as shall be provided by law.

§7. The militia shall, in all cases, except fellony, treason, or breach of the peace, be privileged from arrest during their attendance at musters and elections of officers, and in going to and returning from the same.

§8. The officers and men commissioned and organized, shall not be entitled to, or receive any pay, rations, or emoluments when not in active service.

ARTICLE XI.

EDUCATION.

§1. The common schools, and other educational institutions of the State, shall be under the management of a Board of Education, consisting of a Superintendent of Public Instruction and two members from each Congressional District.

The Governor of the State shall be *ex officio* a member of the Board, but shall have no vote in its proceedings.

§2. The Superintendent of Public Instruction shall be President of the Board of Education, and have the casting vote in case of a tie; he shall have the supervision of the Public Schools of the State, and perform such other duties as may be imposed upon him by the Board and the laws of the State. He shall be elected in the same manner and for the same term as the Governor of the State, and receive such salary as may be fixed by law. An office shall be assigned him in the Capitol of the State.

§3. The members of the Board shall hold office for a term of four years, and until their successors shall be elected and qualified. After the first election under the Constitution, the Board shall be divided into two equal classes, so that each class shall consist of one member from each District. The seats of the first class shall be vacated at the expiration of two years from the day of election, so that one-half may be chosen biennially.

§4. The members of the Board of Education, except the Superintendent, shall be elected by the qualified electors of the Congressional Districts in which they are chosen, at the same time and in the same manner as the members of Congress.

§5 The Board of Education shall exercise full legislative powers in reference to the public educational institutions of the State, and its acts, when approved by the Governor, or when re-enacted by two-thirds of the Board, in case of his disapproval, shall have the force and effect of law, unless repealed by the General Assembly.

§6. It shall be the duty of the Board to establish throughout the State, in each township, or other shool district which it may have created, one or more schools at which all the children of the State, between the ages of five and twenty-one years, may attend free of charge.

§7. No rule or law affecting the general interest of education shall be made by the Board without the concurrence of a majority of its members. The style of all acts of the Board shall be, "Be it enacted by the Board of Education of the State of Alabama."

§8. The Board of Education shall be a body politic and corporate, by the name and style of the Board of Education of the State of Alabama. Said Board shall also be a Board of Regents of the State University, and when sitting as a Board of Regents of the University, shall have power to appoint the President and the faculties thereof.

The President of the Univerity shall be *ex officio* a member of the Board of Regents, but shall have no vote in its proceedings.

§9. The Board of Education shall meet annually at the seat of Government at the same time as the General Assembly, but no session shall continue longer than twenty days, nor shall more than one session be held in the same year, unless authorized by the Governor. The members shall receive the same mileage and daily pay as the members of the General Assembly.

§10. The proceeds of all lands that have been or may be granted by the United States to the State for educational purposes; of the swamp lands; and of all lands or other property given by individuals or appropriated by the State for like purposes; and of all estates of deceased persons who have died without leaving a will or heir; and all moneys which may be paid as an equivalent for exemption from military duty, shall be and remain a perpetual fund, which may be increased but not diminished, and the interest and income of which, together with the rents of all such lands as may remain unsold, and such other means as the General Assembly may provide, shall be inviolably appropriated to educational purposes, and to no other purpose whatever.

§11. In addition to the amount accruing from the above sources, one-fifth of the aggregate annual revenue of the State shall be devoted exclusively to the maintenance of public schools.

§12. The General Assembly may give power to the authorities of the School Districts to levy a Poll Tax on the inhabitants of the District in aid of the General School Fund and for no other purpose.

§13. The General Assembly shall levy a specific annual tax upon all Railroad, Navigation, Banking and Insurance Corporations, and upon all Insurance and Foreign Bank and Exchange Agencies, and upon the profits of Foreign Bank bills issued in this State by any Corporation, partnership or persons, which shall be exclusively devoted to the maintenance of public schools.

§14. The General Assembly shall, as soon as practicable, provide for the establishment of an Agricultural College, and shall appropriate the two hundred and forty thousand acres of land donated to this State for the support of such a college, by the act of Congress, passed July 2d, 1865, or the money or scrip, as the case may be, arising from the sale of said lands or any lands which may hereafter be granted, or appropriated for such purpose, for the support and maintenance of such college or schools, and may make the same a branch of the University of Alabama for instruction in agriculture, in the mechanic arts, and the natural sciences connected therewith, and place the same under the supervision of the Regents of the University.

ARTICLE XII.

INDUSTRIAL RESOURCES.

§1. A Bureau of Industrial Resources shall be established, to be under the management of a commissioner, who shall be elected at the first general election, and shall hold his office for the term of four years.

§2. The Commissioner of Industrial Resources shall collect and condense statistical information concerning the productive industries of the State; and shall make, or cause to be made, a careful, accurate and thorough report upon the agriculture and geology of the State, and annually report such additions as the progress of scientific development and extended explorations may require. He shall, from time to time, disseminate among the people of the State such knowledge as he may deem important, concerning improved machinery and production, and for the promotion of their agricultural, manufacturing and mining interests; and shall send out to the people of the United States and foreign countries, such reports concerning the industrial resources of Alabama, as may best make known the advantages offered by the State to imigrants; and shall perform such other duties as the General Assembly may require.

§3. It shall be the duty of the General Assembly at the first session after the adoption of this Constitution, to pass such laws and regulations as may be necessary for the government and protection of this Bureau, and also to fix and provide for the compensation of the Commissioner.

§4. This Bureau shall be located, and the Commissioner shall reside, at the Capital of the State, and he shall annually make a written or printed report to the Governor of the State, to be laid before the General Assembly at each session.

§5. In case of the death, removal or resignation of the Commissioner, the Governor, with the approval of the Senate, shall have power to appoint a Commissioner for the unexpired term.

ARTICLE XIII.

CORPORATIONS.

§1. Corporations may be formed under general laws, but shall not be created by special act, except for municipal purposes. All general laws and special acts passed pursuant to this section may be altered, amended or repealed.

§2. Dues from Corporations shall be secured by such individual liabilities of the Corporators or other means as may be prescribed by law

§3. Each stockholder in any Corporation shall be liable to the amount of the stock held or owned by him.

§4. The property of Corporations now existing or hereafter created, shall forever be subject to taxation the same as property of individuals, except Corporations for educational and charitable purposes.

§5. No right of way shall be appropriated to the use of any Corporation, until full compensation therefor be first made in money, or secured by a deposit of money to the owner, irrespective of any benefit from any improvement proposed by such Corporation, which compensation shall be ascertained by a jury of twelve men in a court of record, as shall be prescribed by law.

§6. The General Assembly shall not have power to establish or incorporate any bank or banking company, or moneyed institution, for the purpose of issuing bills of credit or bills payable to order or bearer, except under the conditions prescribed in this Constitution.

§7. No bank shall be established, otherwise than under a general banking law, as provided in the first section of this article.

§8. The General Assembly may enact a general banking law, which law shall provide for the registry and countersigning by the Governor of the State, of all paper credit designed to be created as money; and ample collateral security, convertable into specie, or the redemption of the same in gold or silver, shall be required, and such collateral security shall be under the control of such officer or officers as may be prescribed by law.

§9. All bills or notes issued as money, shall be, at all times, redeemable in gold or silver, and no law shall be passed sanctioning, directly or indirectly, the suspension, by any bank or banking company, of specie payment.

§10. Holders of bank notes shall be entitled, in case of insolvency, to preference of payment over all other creditors.

§11. Every bank or banking company shall be required to cease all banking operations within twenty years from the time of its organization, and promptly thereafter to close its business.

§12. No bank shall receive directly, or indirectly, a greater rate of interest than shall be allowed by law to individuals lending money.

§13. The State shall not be a stockholder in any bank, nor shall the credit of the State ever be given or lent to any banking company, association, or corporation, except for the purpose of expediting the construction of railroads, or works of internal improvement, within this State, and the credit of the State shall, in no case be given or lent without the approval of both Houses of the General Assembly.

§14. All Corporations shall have the right to sue and shall be subject to be sued, in all courts in like cases as natural persons.

§15. It shall be the duty of the General Assembly to provide for the organization of cities, and incorporated towns, and to restrict their power of taxation, assessments and contracting of debt.

ARTICLE XIV.

EXEMPTED PROPERTY.

§1. The personal property of any resident of this State to the value of one thousand dollars, to be selected by such resident, shall be exempted from sale on execution or other final process of any court issued for the collection of any debt contracted after the adoption of this Constitution.

§2. Every homestead not exceeding eighty acres of land, and the dwelling and appurtenances thereon, to be selected by theowner thereof, and not in any town, city, or village, or in lieu thereof, at the option of the owner, any lot in a city, town, or village, with the dwelling and appurtenances thereon, owned and occupied by any resident of this State, and not exceeding the value of two thousand dollars, shall be exempted from sale, on execution, or any other final process from a court, from any debt contracted after the adoption of this Constitution. Such exemption, however, shall not extend to any mortgage lawfully obtained, but such mortgage or other alienation of such homestead, by the owner thereof, if a married man, shall not be valid without the voluntary signature and assent of the the wife of the same.

§3. The homestead of a family, after the death of the owner thereof, shall be exempt from the payment of any debts contracted after the adoption of this Constitution, in all cases, during the minority of the children.

§4. The provisions of Sections one and two of this Article shall not be so construed as to prevent a laborer's lien for work done and performed for the person claiming such exemption, or a mechanic's lien for work done on the premises.

§5 If the owner of a homestead die, leaving a widow, but no children, the same shall be exempt, and the rents and profits thereof shall inure to her benefit.

§6. The real and personal property of any female in this State, acquired before marriage, and all property, real and personal, to which she may afterwards be entitled by gift, grant, inheritance or devise, shall be and remain the separate estate and property of such female, and shall not be liable for any debts, obligations, and engagements of her husband, and may be devised or bequeathed by her, the same as if she were a *femme sole*.

ARTICLE XV.

OATH OF OFFICE.

§1. All civil officers of this State, Legislative, Executive and Judicial, before they enter upon the execution of the duties of their respective offices, shall take the following oath :

"I, A, B., do solemnly swear, or affirm, that I am not disfranchised by the Constitution of Alabama, or by the Constitution or laws of the United States ; that I will honestly and faithfully support and defend the Constitution and laws of the United States, the Union of the States, and the Constitution and laws of the State of Alabama, so long as I remain a citizen thereof ; and that I will honestly and faithfully discharge the duties of the office upon which I am about to enter to the best of my ability, So help me God."

ARTICLE XVI.

AMENDMENTS TO THE CONSTITUTION.

§1. The General Assembly, whenever two-thirds of each House shall deem it necessary, may propose amendments to this Constitution, which proposed amendments shall be duly published in print at least three months before the next general election of Representatives, for the consideration of the people; and it shall be the duty of the several returning officers at the next general election which shall be held for Representatives, to open a poll for, and make a return, to the Secretary of State for the time being, of the names of all those voting for Representatives who have voted on such proposed amendments, and if thereupon it shall appear that a majority of all the citizens of the State voting for Representatives, have voted in favor of such proposed amendmənts, and two-thirds of each House of the next General Assembly shall, after such an election, and before another, ratify the same amendments, by yeas and nays, they shall be valid to all intents and purposes, as part of this Consitution : Provided, that the said proposed amendments shall at each of the said sessions, have been read three times on three several days in each House.

After the expiration of twelve months from the adoption of this Constitution, no Convention shall be held for the purpose of altering or amending the Constitntion of this State, unless the question of Convention or no Convention shall be first submitted to a vote of all the electors, twenty-one years of age and upwards, and approved by a majority of the electors voting at said election.

E. W. PECK, President.

ROBERT BARBER, Secretary.

A. J. Applegate,	Thomas Adams,	W. A. Austin,	B. Alexander,
J. H. Autrey,	D. H. Bingham,	W. T. Blackford,	A. Bingham,
M. D. Brainard,	Sam. Blandon,	W. Buckley,	A. E. Buck,
J. H. Burdick,	C. W. Buckley,	J. Carraway,	P. Burton,
J. Collins,	D. E. Coon,	J. H. Davis,	Thomas Diggs,
G. J. Dykes,	George Ely,	P. Finley,	S. S. Gardner,
W. C. Garrison,	O. Gregory,	J. K. Greene,	A. Griffin,
J. M. Hatcher,	T. Haughey,	C. Hayes,	B. Inge,
W. Johnson,	A. W. Jones,	C. Jones,	J. C. Keffer,
S. F. Kennamer,	Tom Lee,	D. Lore,	H. McGown,
J. Mahan,	J. W. McLeod,	B. O. Masterson,	J. J. Martin,
S. Moore,	C. A. Miller,	J. F. Morton,	A. L. Morgan,
T. M. Peters,	B. W. Norris,	H. C. Russell,	J. T. Rapier,
J. Silsby,	B. F. Saffold,	L. R. Smith,	Wm. Skinner,
H. J. Springfield,	C. L. Steed,	J. P. Stow,	L. B. Strange,
W. A. Walker,	C. O. Whitney,	J. R. Walker,	J. W. Wilhite,
J. A. Yordy,	R. M. Reynolds,	N. D. Stamwood.	

PRINTED AT THE GREAT REPUBLIC OFFICE, WASHINGTON, D. C.

www.ingramcontent.com/pod-product-compliance
Lightning Source LLC
LaVergne TN
LVHW020643110826
845149LV00004B/1330
* 9 7 8 1 4 1 8 1 9 0 3 1 6 *